D1441974

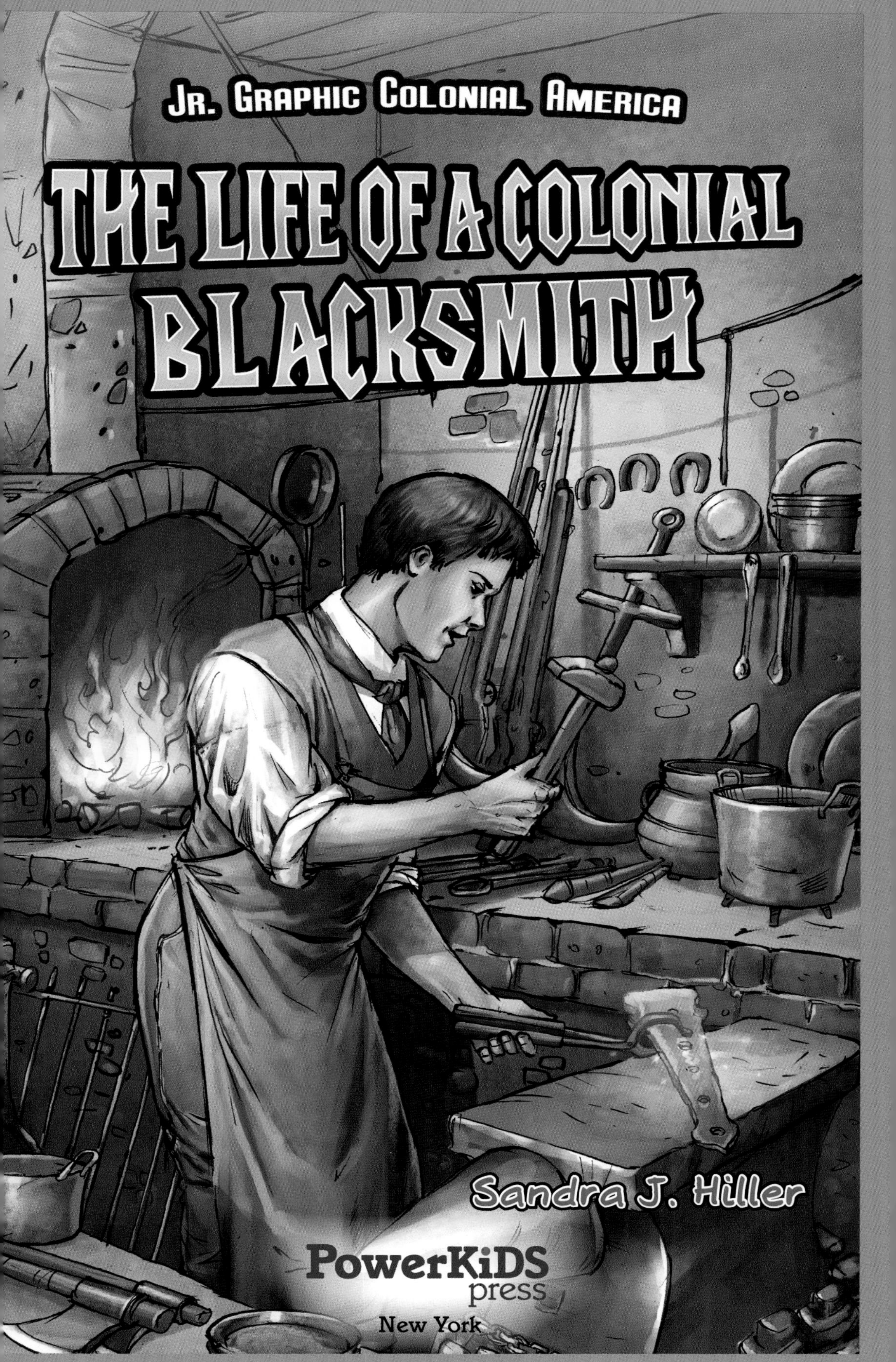

Jr. Graphic Colonial America

The Life of a Colonial Blacksmith

Sandra J. Hiller

PowerKiDS press
New York

Published in 2014 by The Rosen Publishing Group, Inc.
29 East 21st Street, New York, NY 10010

Note: The main characters in this book were real-life colonists who held
the jobs described. In some cases, not much else is known about their lives.
When necessary, we have used the best available historical scholarship on the
professions and daily life in colonial America to create as full and accurate a
portrayal as possible.

First Edition

Editor: Joanne Randolph
Book Design: Planman Technologies
Illustrations: Planman Technologies

Library of Congress Cataloging-in-Publication Data

Hiller, Sandra J., 1956-
  The life of a colonial blacksmith / by Sandra J. Hiller. — First edition.
    pages cm. — (Jr. graphic colonial America)
  Includes index.
  ISBN 978-1-4777-1308-2 (library binding) — ISBN 978-1-4777-1433-1 (pbk.)
  — ISBN 978-1-4777-1434-8 (6-pack)
  1. Blacksmithing—United States—History—18th century—Juvenile literature.
  2. Blacksmiths—United States—History—18th century—Juvenile literature.
  3. Blacksmithing—United States—History—18th century—Comic books, strips,
  etc. 4. Blacksmiths—United States—History—18th century—Comic books,
  strips, etc. 5. Graphic novels. I. Title.
  TT220.H39 2014
  682.0973—dc23
                                                              2012048603

Manufactured in the United States of America
CPSIA Compliance Information: Batch #S13PK1: For Further Information contact Rosen Publishing, New York,
New York at 1-800-237-9932

Contents

Introduction

Colonial **blacksmiths** did much more than just shoe horses for their fellow settlers in the English colonies. The blacksmith was a key member of colonial society. Blacksmiths repaired the tools, cooking equipment, and many of the weapons colonists needed. Colonial blacksmiths also made tools and equipment, including axes for farmers and traders, and latches, hinges, and nails for homes. By making tools and later, weapons, for the colonists, colonial blacksmiths helped the American colonies become independent.

Jeremiah Williams and his son Edward were colonial Boston blacksmiths. They came from a patriotic family. Little else is known about them, but we can envision how they spent their days.

Main Characters

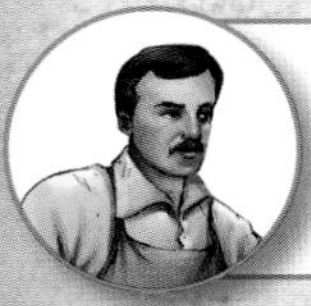

Jeremiah Williams (c. 1700s) A middle-aged blacksmith who owns his own blacksmith shop.

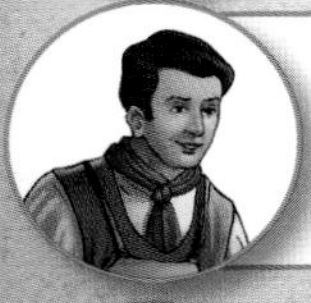

Edward Williams (1746–1777) A **journeyman** blacksmith, the son of Jeremiah Williams.

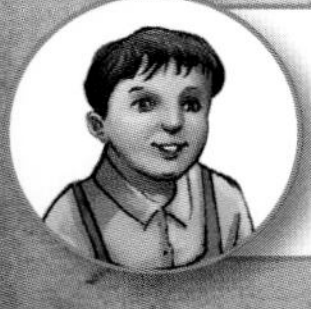

Garrett The newest **apprentice** blacksmith, a 10-year-old whose father signs an agreement with Jeremiah Williams.

The Life of a Colonial Blacksmith

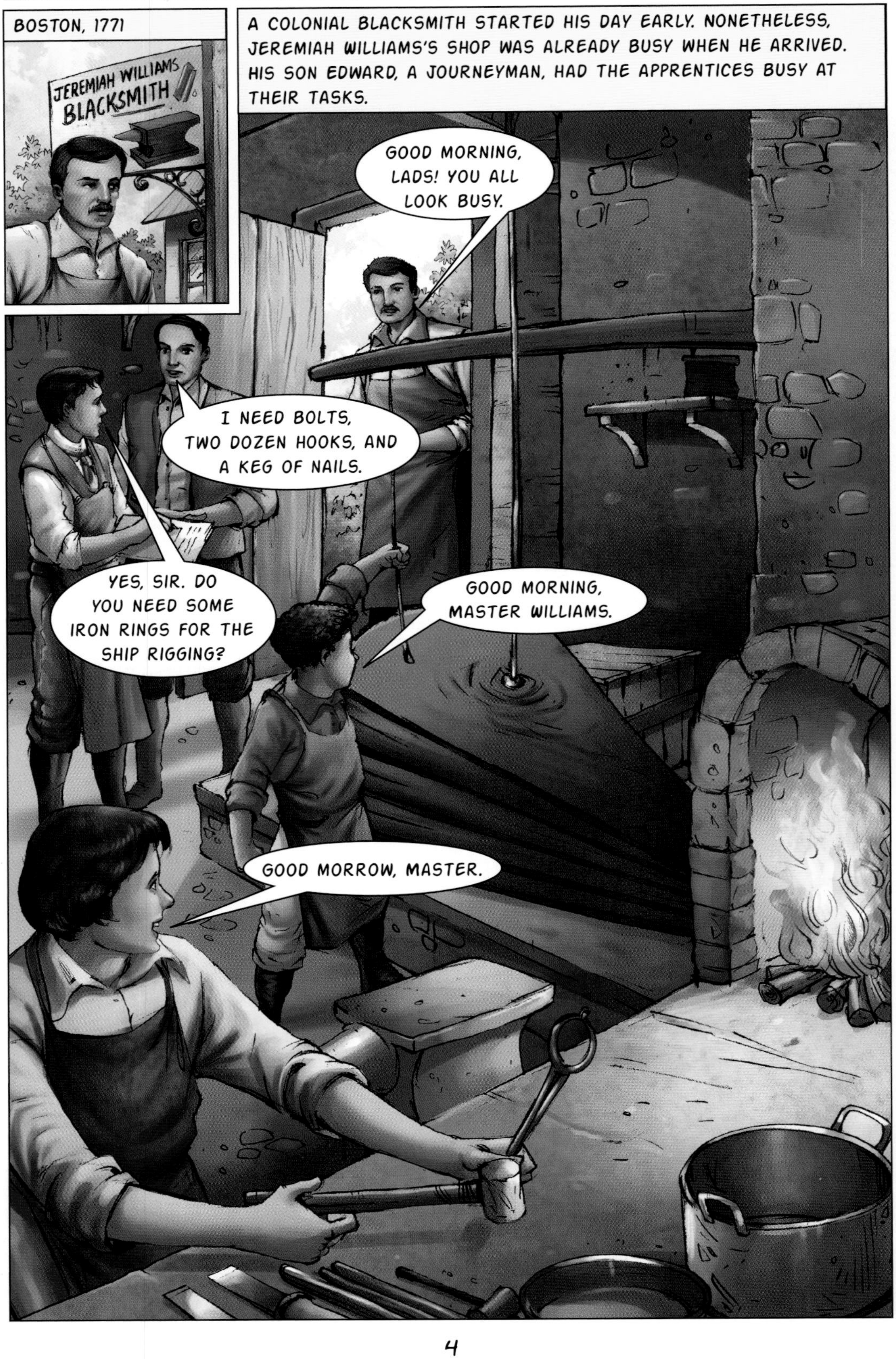

BOSTON, 1771
JEREMIAH WILLIAMS BLACKSMITH
A COLONIAL BLACKSMITH STARTED HIS DAY EARLY. NONETHELESS, JEREMIAH WILLIAMS'S SHOP WAS ALREADY BUSY WHEN HE ARRIVED. HIS SON EDWARD, A JOURNEYMAN, HAD THE APPRENTICES BUSY AT THEIR TASKS.
GOOD MORNING, LADS! YOU ALL LOOK BUSY.
I NEED BOLTS, TWO DOZEN HOOKS, AND A KEG OF NAILS.
YES, SIR. DO YOU NEED SOME IRON RINGS FOR THE SHIP RIGGING?
GOOD MORNING, MASTER WILLIAMS.
GOOD MORROW, MASTER.

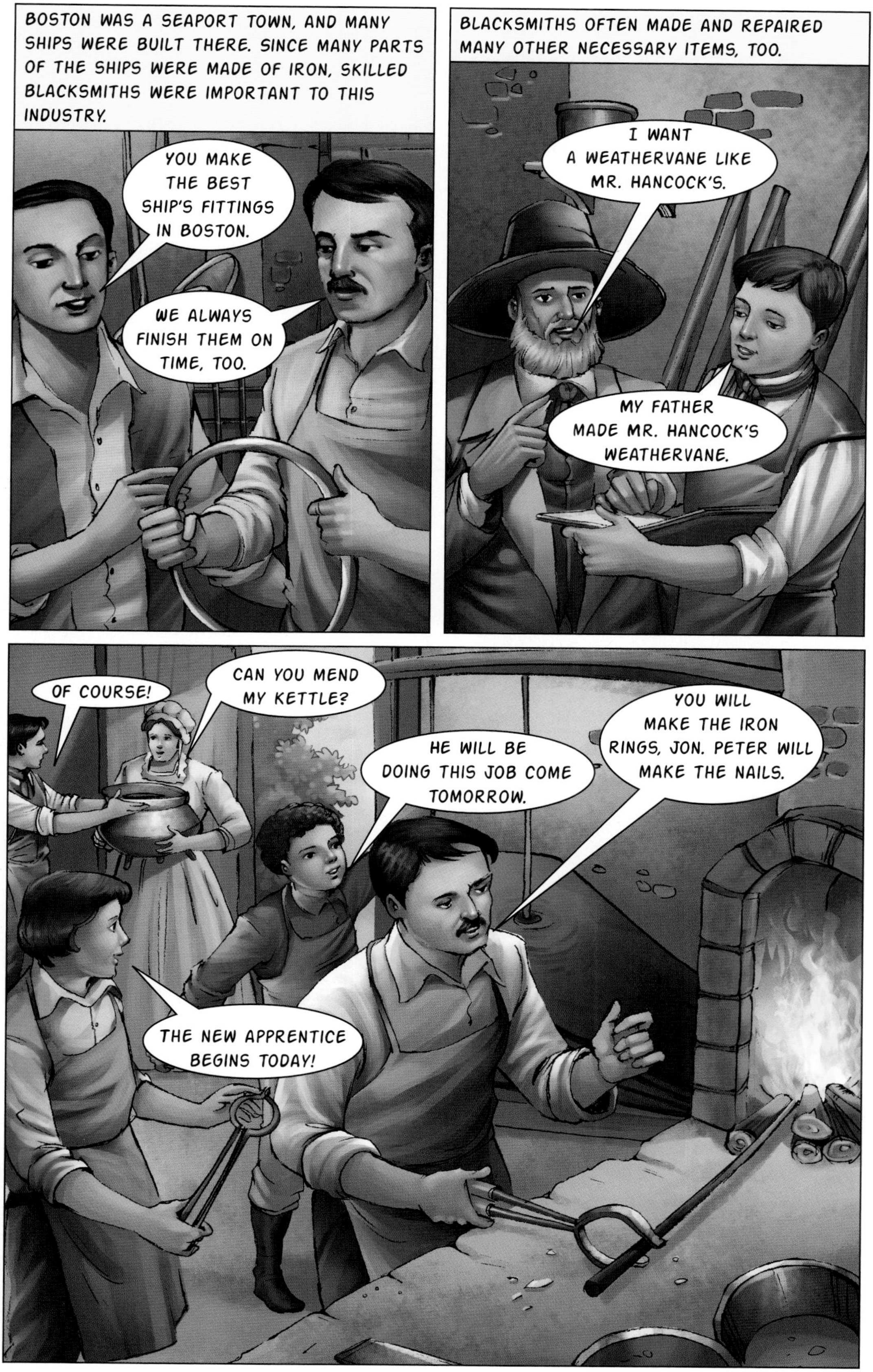
BOSTON WAS A SEAPORT TOWN, AND MANY SHIPS WERE BUILT THERE. SINCE MANY PARTS OF THE SHIPS WERE MADE OF IRON, SKILLED BLACKSMITHS WERE IMPORTANT TO THIS INDUSTRY.
YOU MAKE THE BEST SHIP'S FITTINGS IN BOSTON.
WE ALWAYS FINISH THEM ON TIME, TOO.
BLACKSMITHS OFTEN MADE AND REPAIRED MANY OTHER NECESSARY ITEMS, TOO.
I WANT A WEATHERVANE LIKE MR. HANCOCK'S.
MY FATHER MADE MR. HANCOCK'S WEATHERVANE.
CAN YOU MEND MY KETTLE?
OF COURSE!
YOU WILL MAKE THE IRON RINGS, JON. PETER WILL MAKE THE NAILS.
HE WILL BE DOING THIS JOB COME TOMORROW.
THE NEW APPRENTICE BEGINS TODAY!

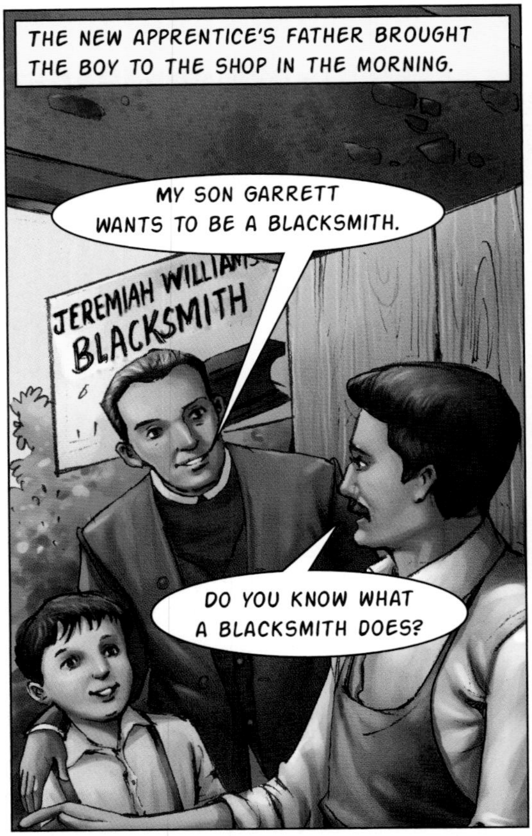
THE NEW APPRENTICE'S FATHER BROUGHT THE BOY TO THE SHOP IN THE MORNING.
MY SON GARRETT WANTS TO BE A BLACKSMITH.
JEREMIAH WILLIAMS BLACKSMITH
DO YOU KNOW WHAT A BLACKSMITH DOES?

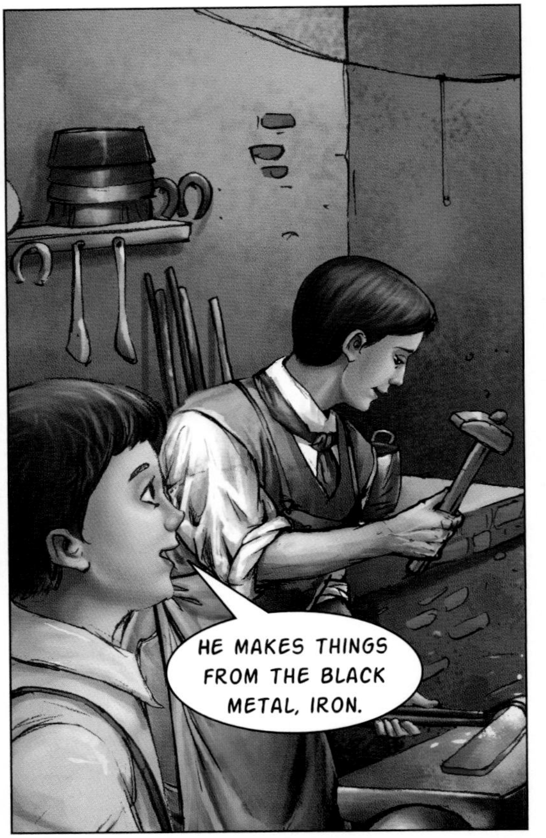
HE MAKES THINGS FROM THE BLACK METAL, IRON.

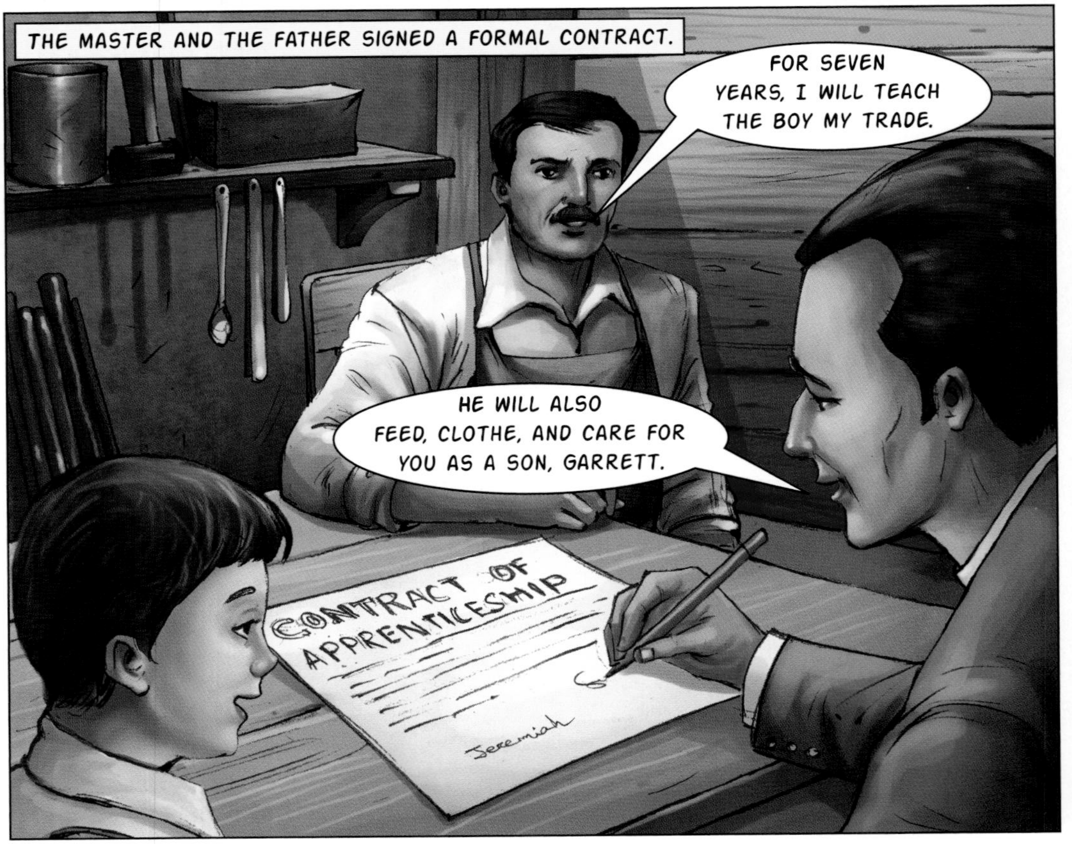
THE MASTER AND THE FATHER SIGNED A FORMAL CONTRACT.
FOR SEVEN YEARS, I WILL TEACH THE BOY MY TRADE.
HE WILL ALSO FEED, CLOTHE, AND CARE FOR YOU AS A SON, GARRETT.
CONTRACT OF APPRENTICESHIP
Jeremiah

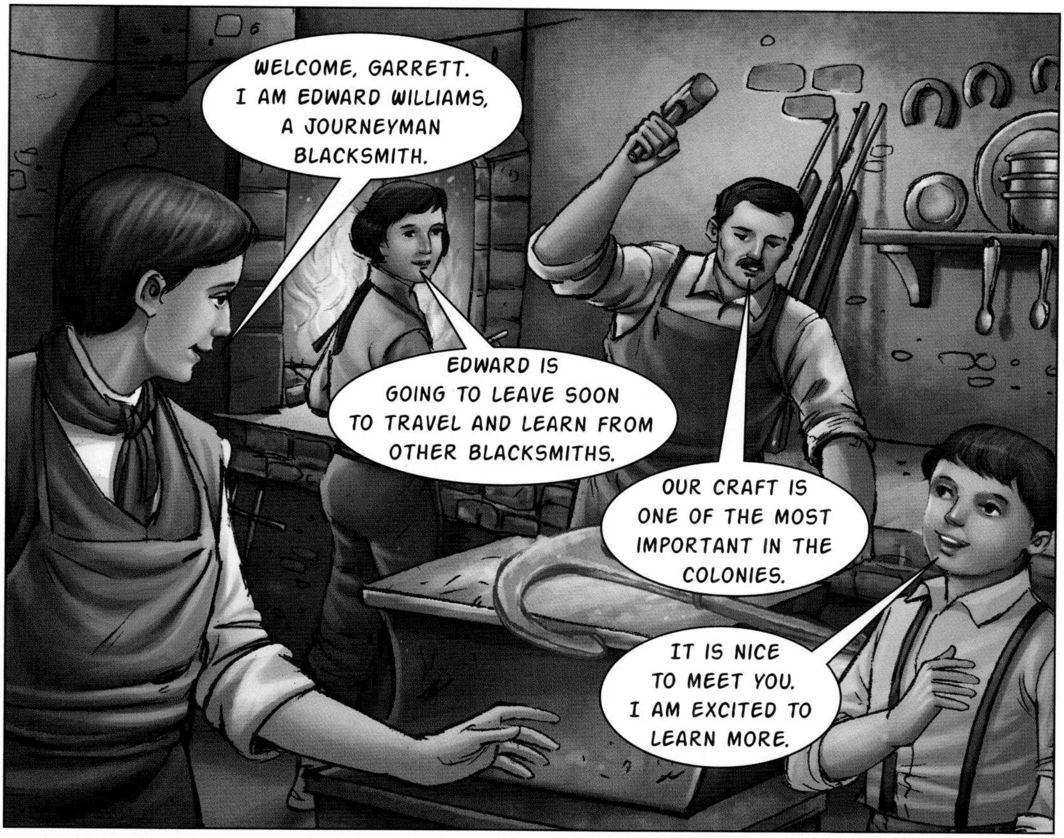
WELCOME, GARRETT. I AM EDWARD WILLIAMS, A JOURNEYMAN BLACKSMITH.
EDWARD IS GOING TO LEAVE SOON TO TRAVEL AND LEARN FROM OTHER BLACKSMITHS.
OUR CRAFT IS ONE OF THE MOST IMPORTANT IN THE COLONIES.
IT IS NICE TO MEET YOU. I AM EXCITED TO LEARN MORE.

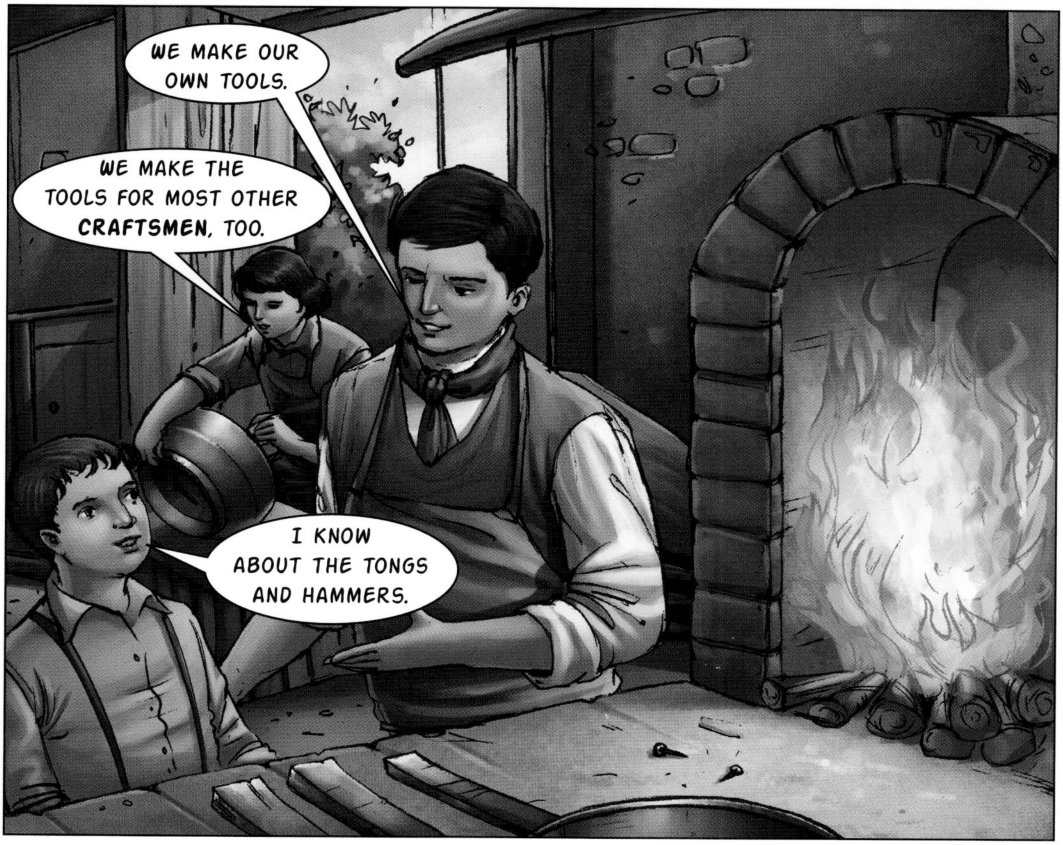
WE MAKE OUR OWN TOOLS.
WE MAKE THE TOOLS FOR MOST OTHER **CRAFTSMEN**, TOO.
I KNOW ABOUT THE TONGS AND HAMMERS.

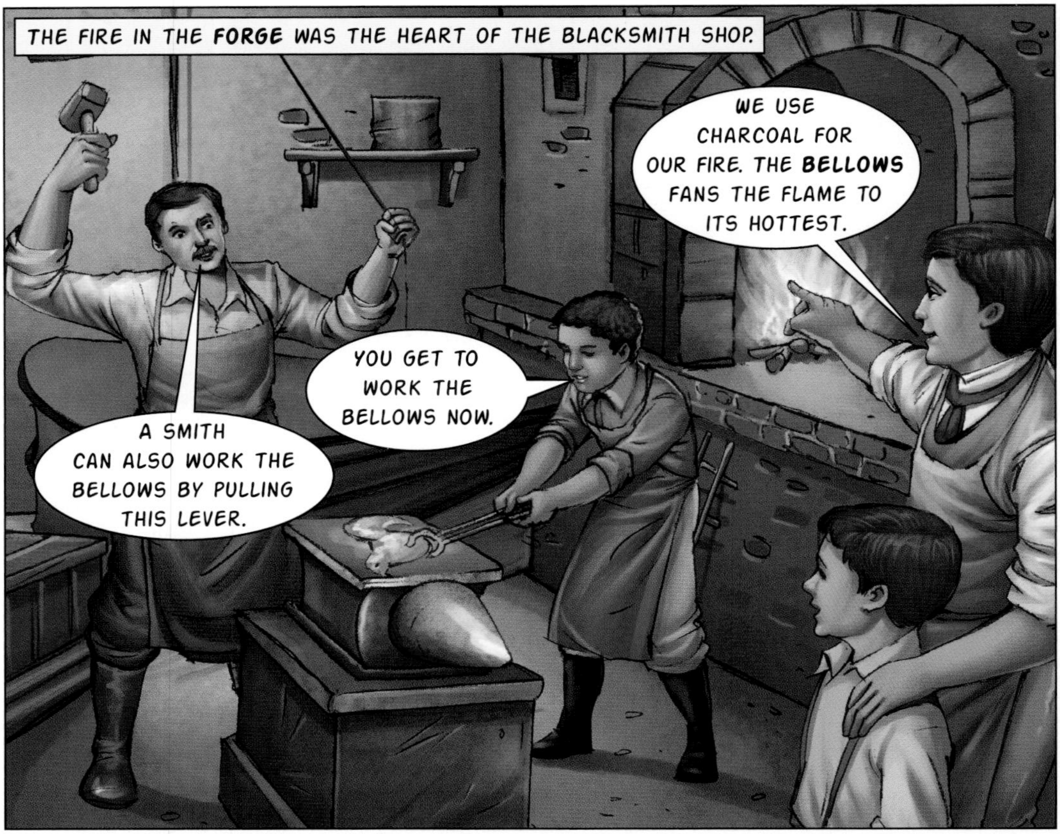
THE FIRE IN THE FORGE WAS THE HEART OF THE BLACKSMITH SHOP.
WE USE CHARCOAL FOR OUR FIRE. THE BELLOWS FANS THE FLAME TO ITS HOTTEST.
YOU GET TO WORK THE BELLOWS NOW.
A SMITH CAN ALSO WORK THE BELLOWS BY PULLING THIS LEVER.

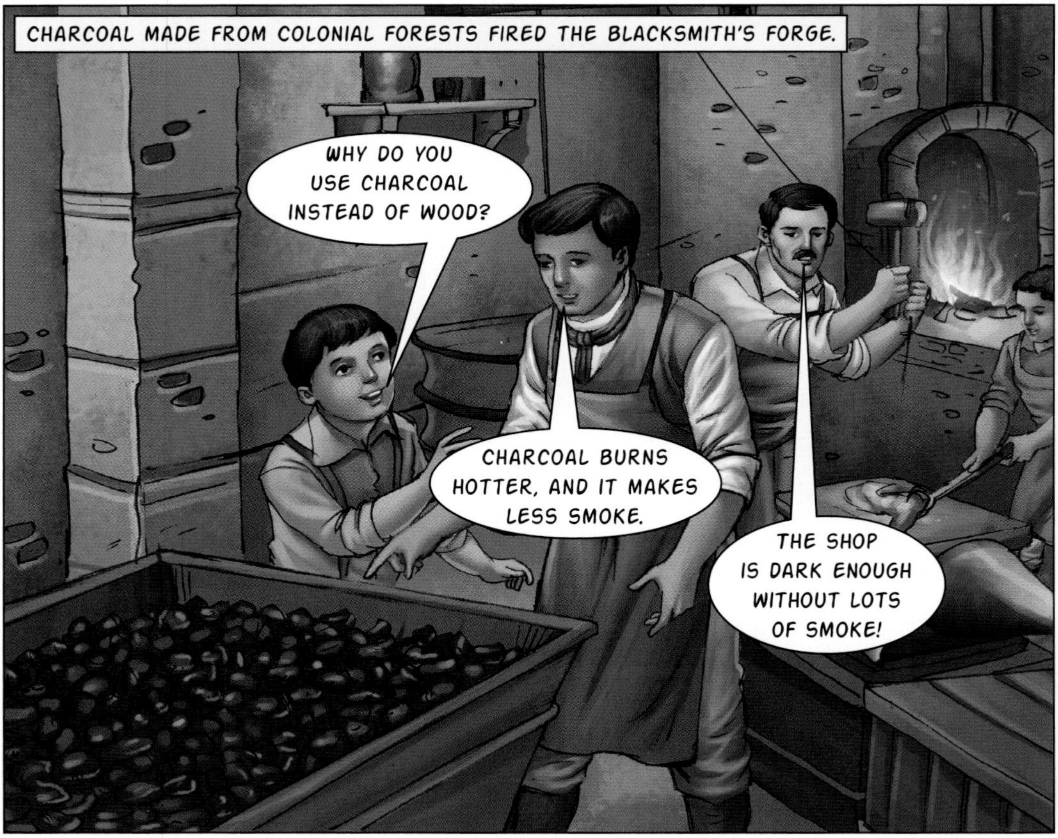
CHARCOAL MADE FROM COLONIAL FORESTS FIRED THE BLACKSMITH'S FORGE.
WHY DO YOU USE CHARCOAL INSTEAD OF WOOD?
CHARCOAL BURNS HOTTER, AND IT MAKES LESS SMOKE.
THE SHOP IS DARK ENOUGH WITHOUT LOTS OF SMOKE!

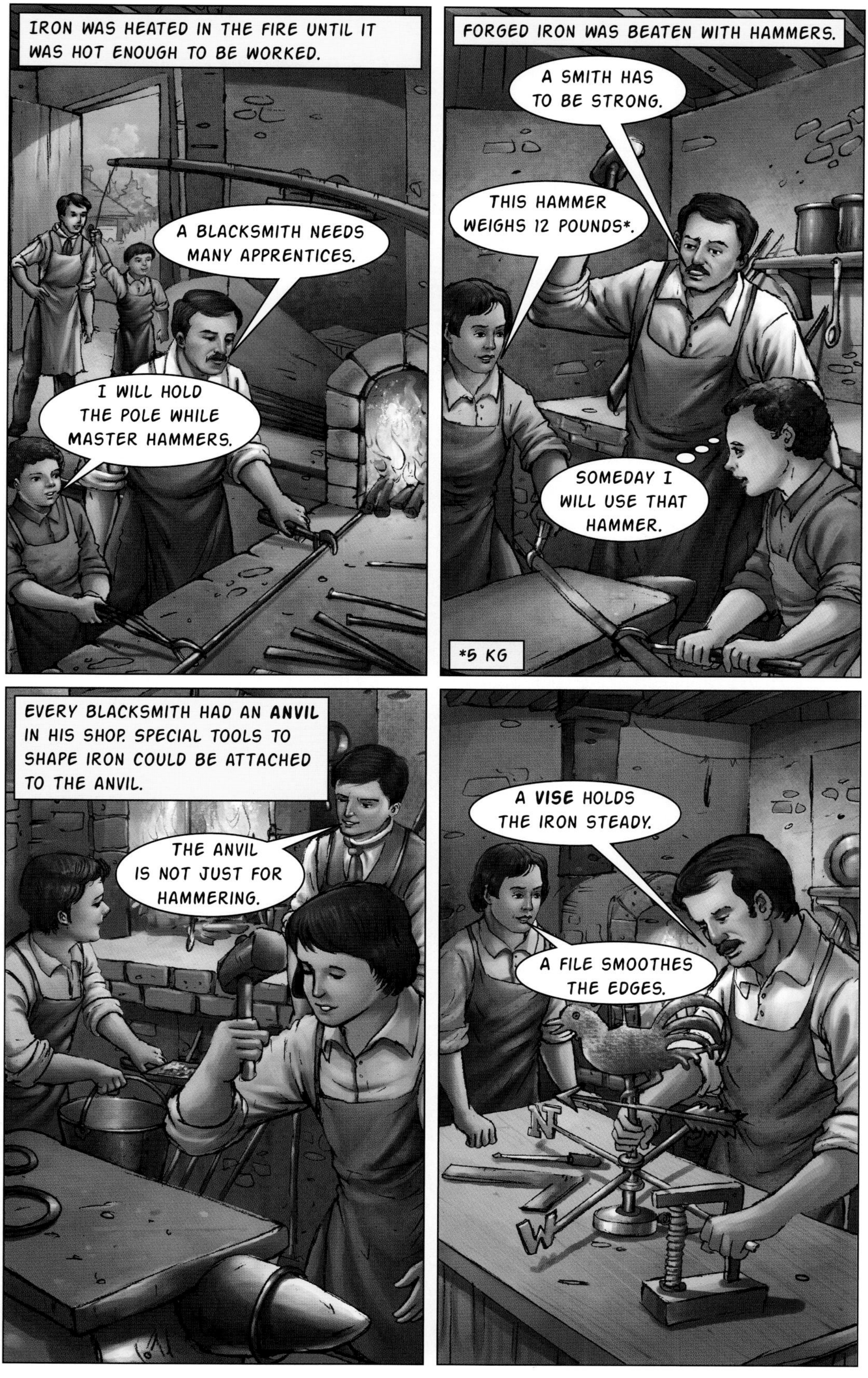

IRON WAS HEATED IN THE FIRE UNTIL IT WAS HOT ENOUGH TO BE WORKED.
A BLACKSMITH NEEDS MANY APPRENTICES.
I WILL HOLD THE POLE WHILE MASTER HAMMERS.
FORGED IRON WAS BEATEN WITH HAMMERS.
A SMITH HAS TO BE STRONG.
THIS HAMMER WEIGHS 12 POUNDS*.
SOMEDAY I WILL USE THAT HAMMER.
*5 KG
EVERY BLACKSMITH HAD AN **ANVIL** IN HIS SHOP. SPECIAL TOOLS TO SHAPE IRON COULD BE ATTACHED TO THE ANVIL.
THE ANVIL IS NOT JUST FOR HAMMERING.
A **VISE** HOLDS THE IRON STEADY.
A FILE SMOOTHES THE EDGES.

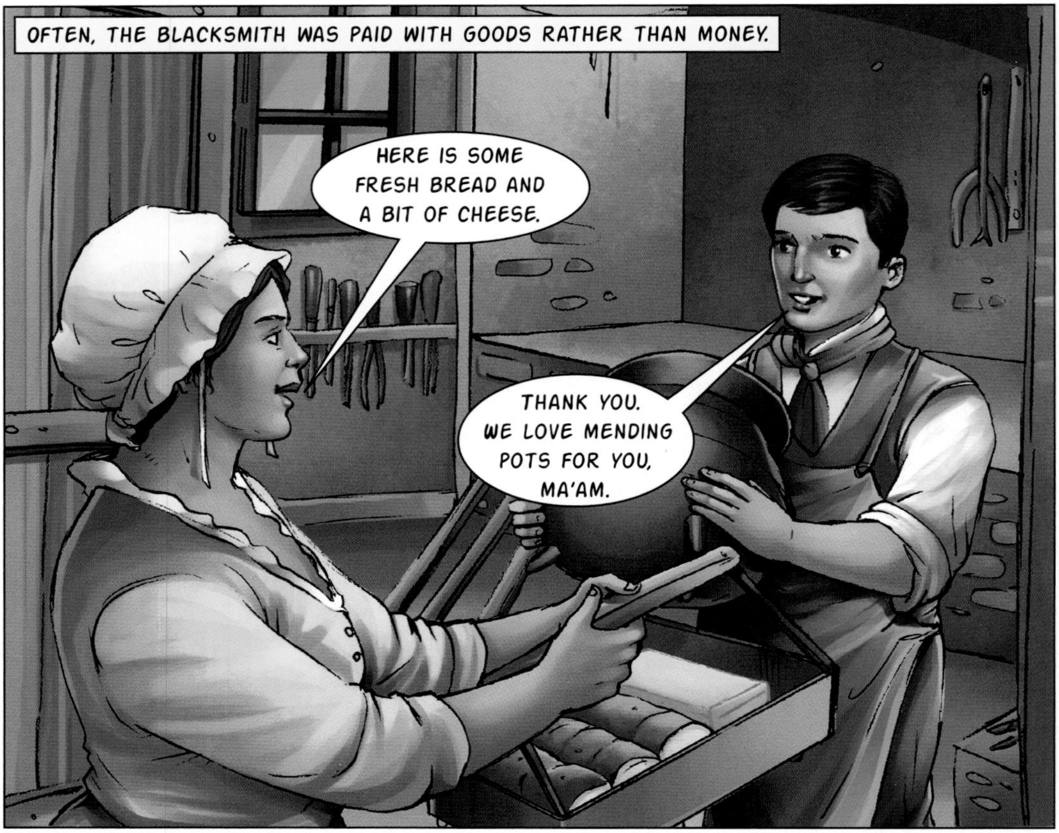
OFTEN, THE BLACKSMITH WAS PAID WITH GOODS RATHER THAN MONEY.
HERE IS SOME FRESH BREAD AND A BIT OF CHEESE.
THANK YOU. WE LOVE MENDING POTS FOR YOU, MA'AM.

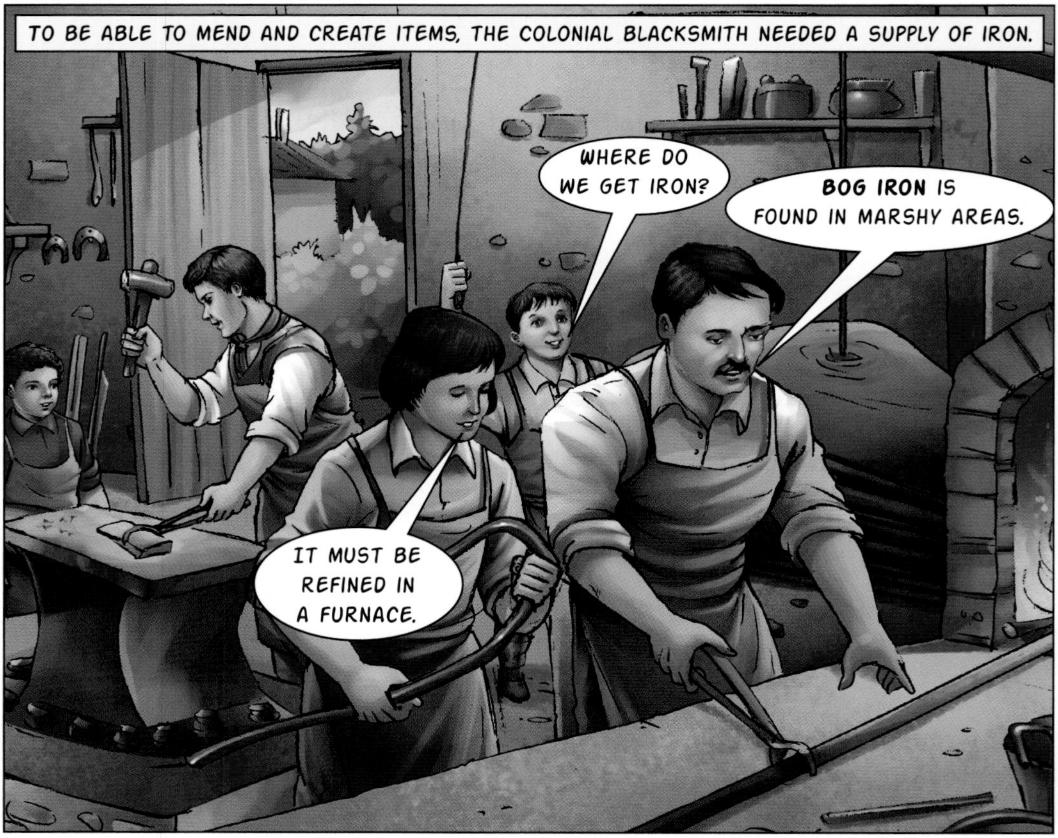
TO BE ABLE TO MEND AND CREATE ITEMS, THE COLONIAL BLACKSMITH NEEDED A SUPPLY OF IRON.
WHERE DO WE GET IRON?
BOG IRON IS FOUND IN MARSHY AREAS.
IT MUST BE REFINED IN A FURNACE.

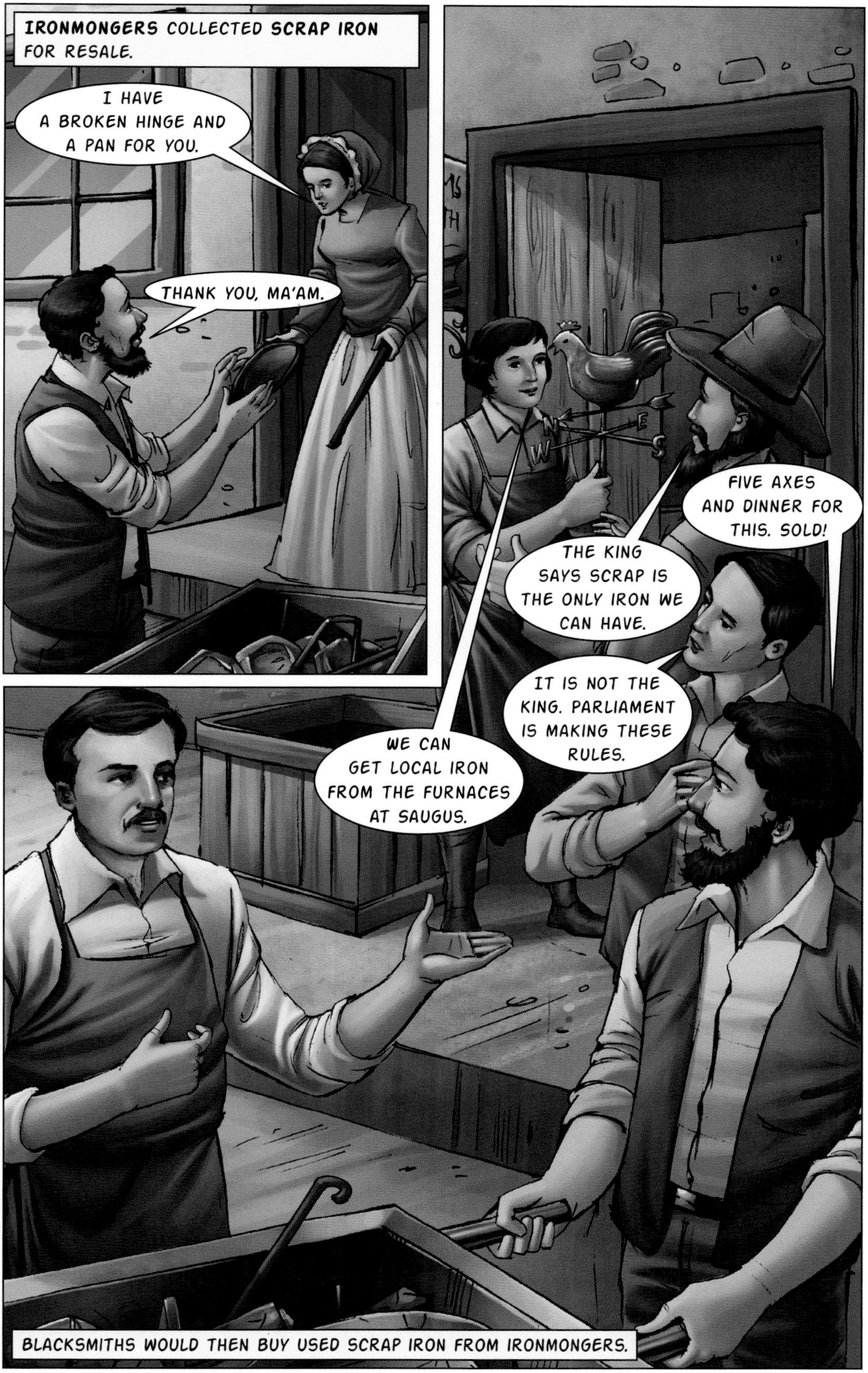
IRONMONGERS COLLECTED SCRAP IRON FOR RESALE.
I HAVE A BROKEN HINGE AND A PAN FOR YOU.
THANK YOU, MA'AM.
FIVE AXES AND DINNER FOR THIS. SOLD!
THE KING SAYS SCRAP IS THE ONLY IRON WE CAN HAVE.
IT IS NOT THE KING. PARLIAMENT IS MAKING THESE RULES.
WE CAN GET LOCAL IRON FROM THE FURNACES AT SAUGUS.
BLACKSMITHS WOULD THEN BUY USED SCRAP IRON FROM IRONMONGERS.

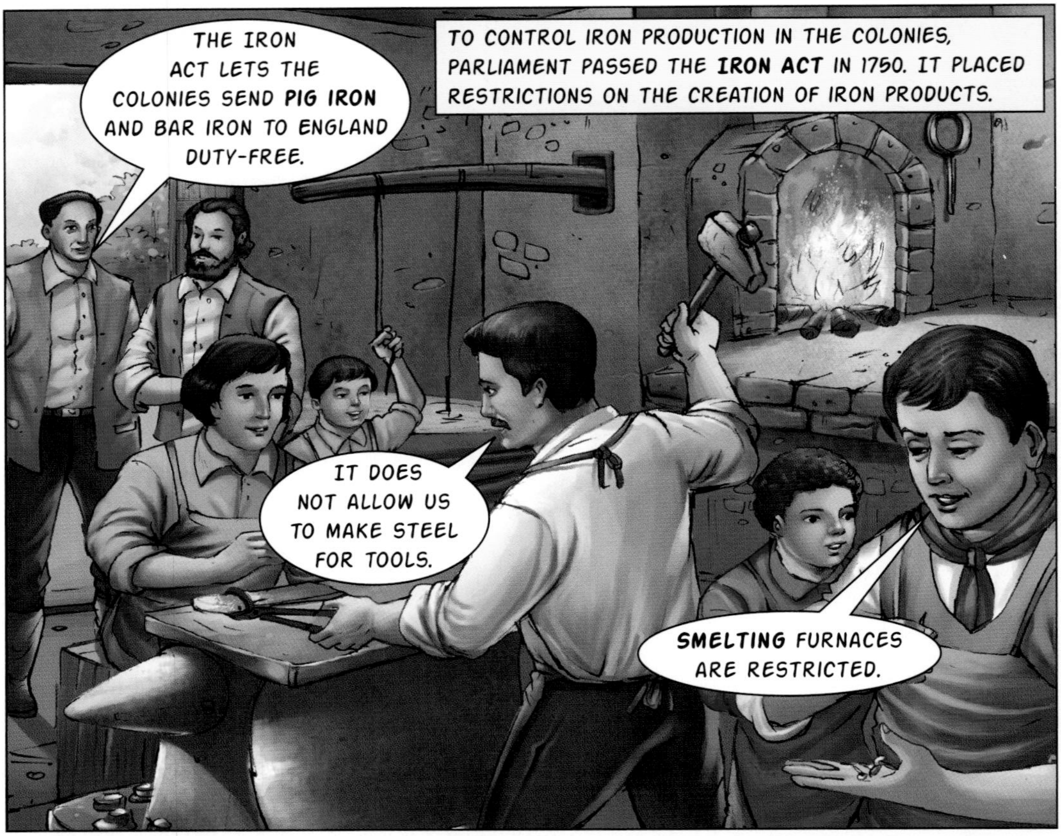
TO CONTROL IRON PRODUCTION IN THE COLONIES, PARLIAMENT PASSED THE **IRON ACT** IN 1750. IT PLACED RESTRICTIONS ON THE CREATION OF IRON PRODUCTS.
THE IRON ACT LETS THE COLONIES SEND **PIG IRON** AND BAR IRON TO ENGLAND DUTY-FREE.
IT DOES NOT ALLOW US TO MAKE STEEL FOR TOOLS.
SMELTING FURNACES ARE RESTRICTED.

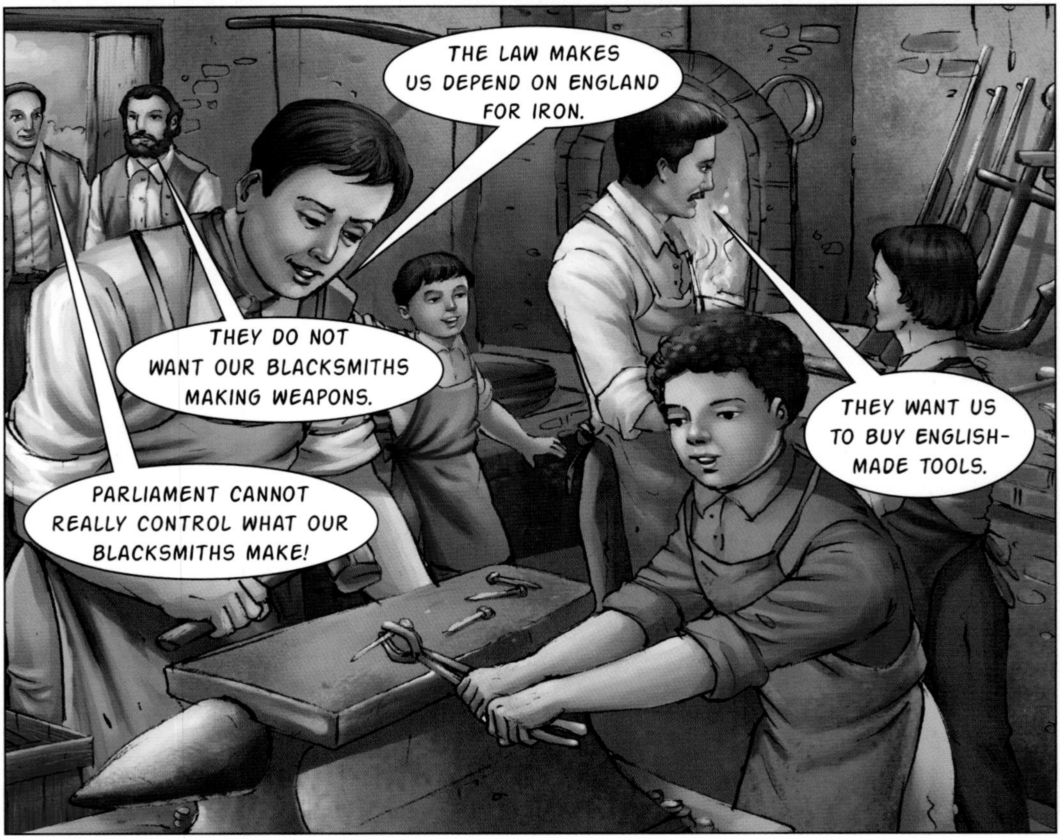
THE LAW MAKES US DEPEND ON ENGLAND FOR IRON.
THEY DO NOT WANT OUR BLACKSMITHS MAKING WEAPONS.
THEY WANT US TO BUY ENGLISH-MADE TOOLS.
PARLIAMENT CANNOT REALLY CONTROL WHAT OUR BLACKSMITHS MAKE!

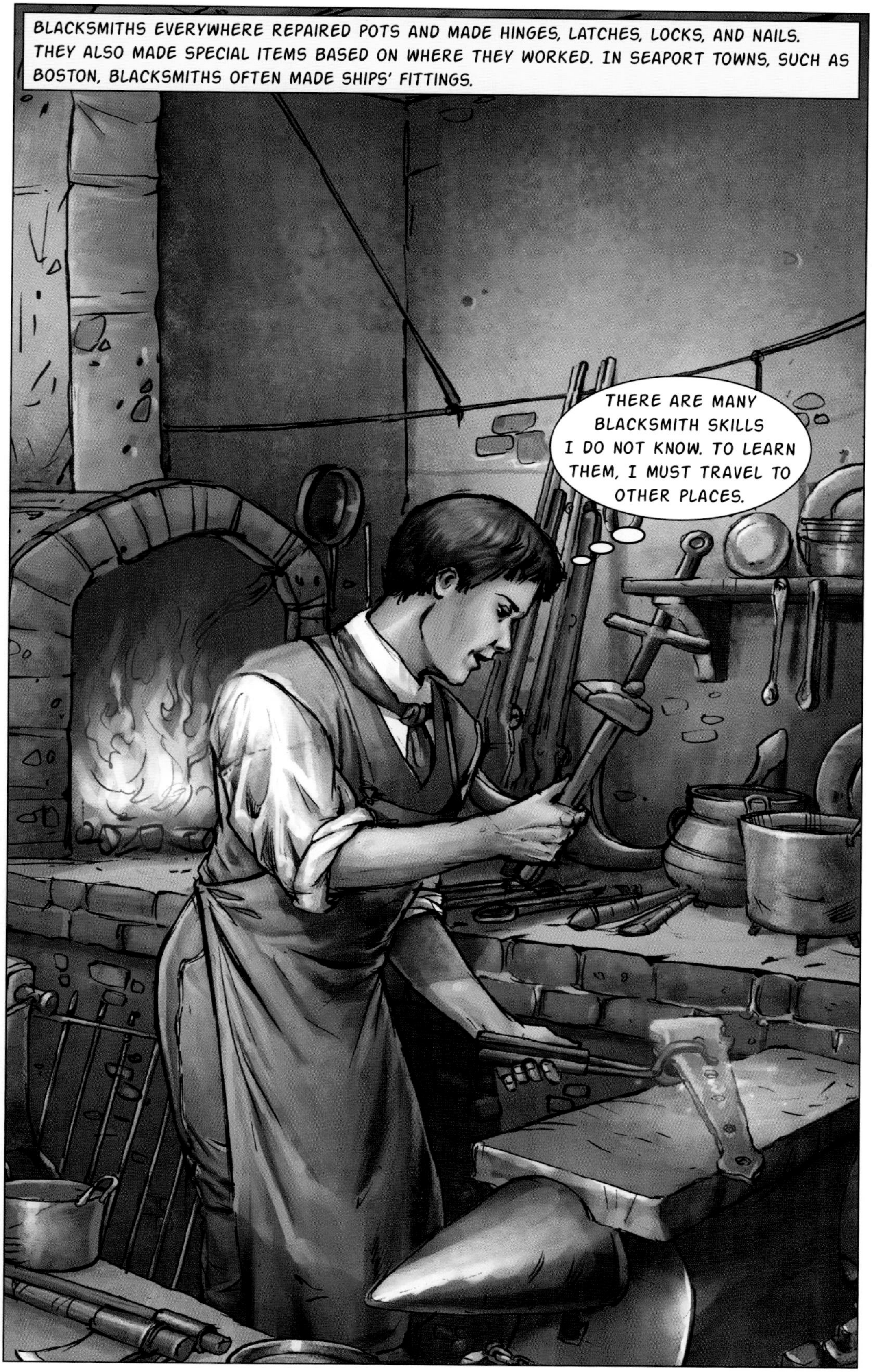
BLACKSMITHS EVERYWHERE REPAIRED POTS AND MADE HINGES, LATCHES, LOCKS, AND NAILS. THEY ALSO MADE SPECIAL ITEMS BASED ON WHERE THEY WORKED. IN SEAPORT TOWNS, SUCH AS BOSTON, BLACKSMITHS OFTEN MADE SHIPS' FITTINGS.
THERE ARE MANY BLACKSMITH SKILLS I DO NOT KNOW. TO LEARN THEM, I MUST TRAVEL TO OTHER PLACES.

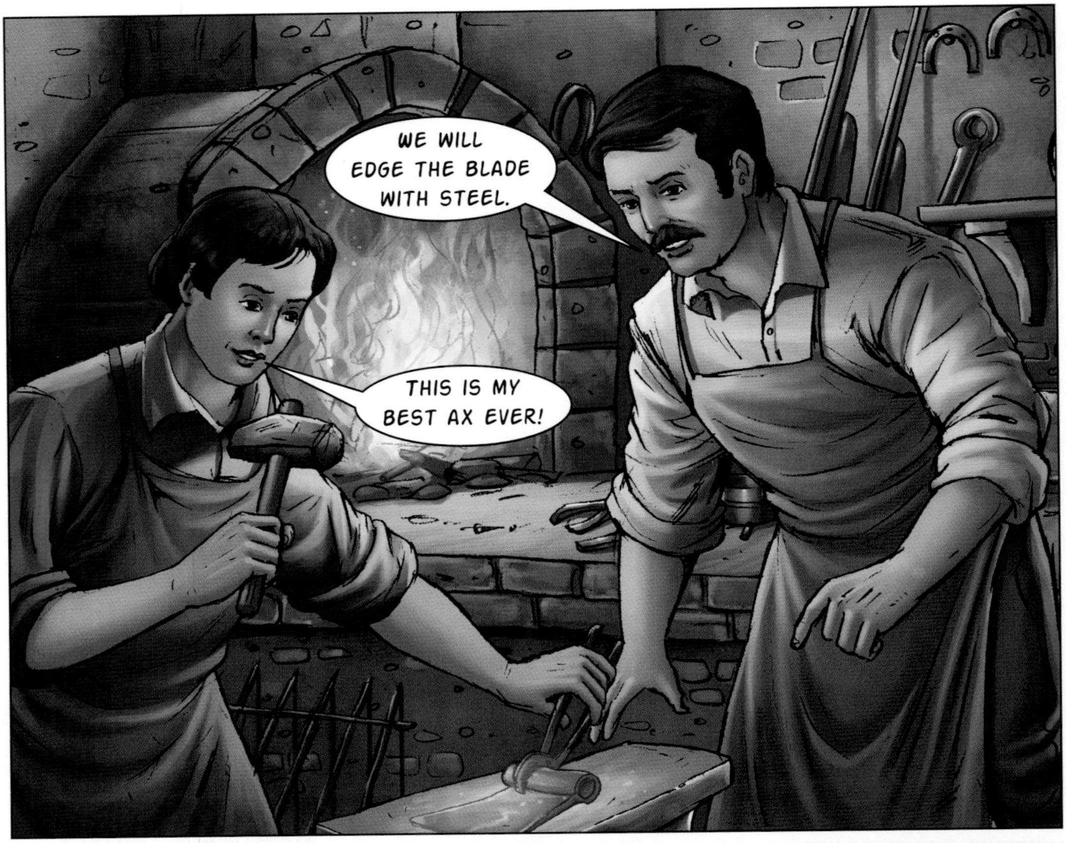
WE WILL EDGE THE BLADE WITH STEEL.
THIS IS MY BEST AX EVER!

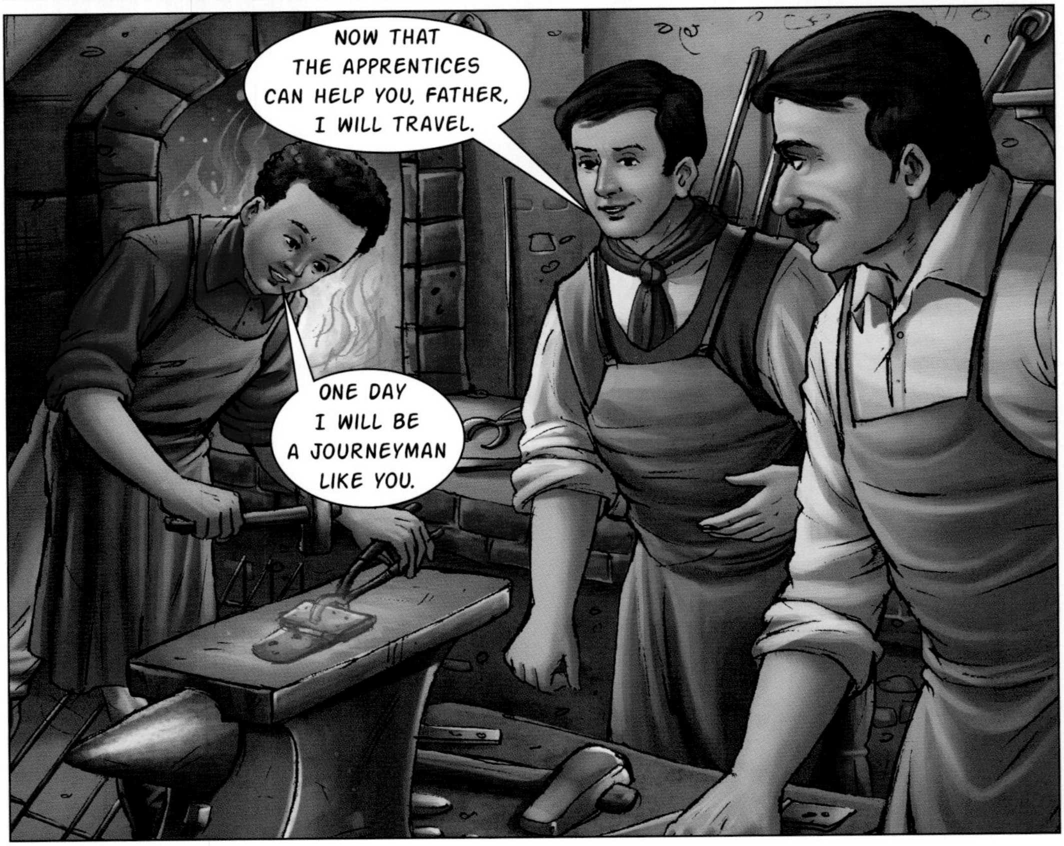
NOW THAT THE APPRENTICES CAN HELP YOU, FATHER, I WILL TRAVEL.
ONE DAY I WILL BE A JOURNEYMAN LIKE YOU.

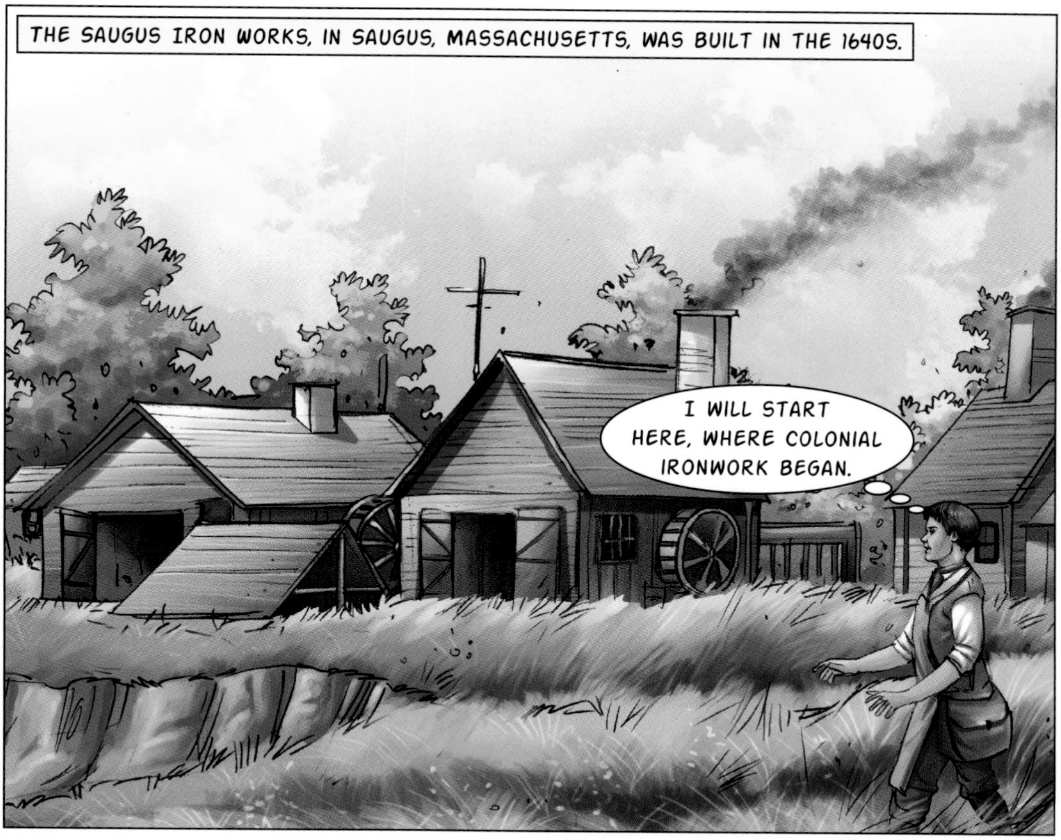
THE SAUGUS IRON WORKS, IN SAUGUS, MASSACHUSETTS, WAS BUILT IN THE 1640S.
I WILL START HERE, WHERE COLONIAL IRONWORK BEGAN.

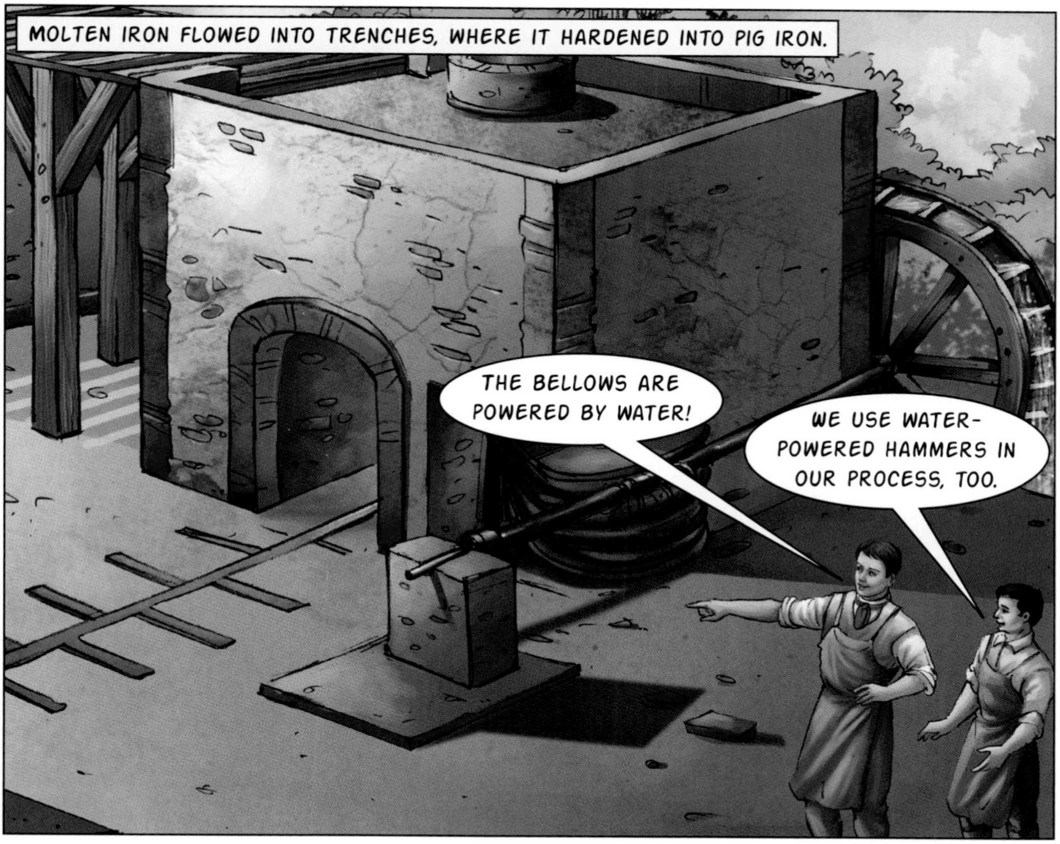
MOLTEN IRON FLOWED INTO TRENCHES, WHERE IT HARDENED INTO PIG IRON.
THE BELLOWS ARE POWERED BY WATER!
WE USE WATER-POWERED HAMMERS IN OUR PROCESS, TOO.

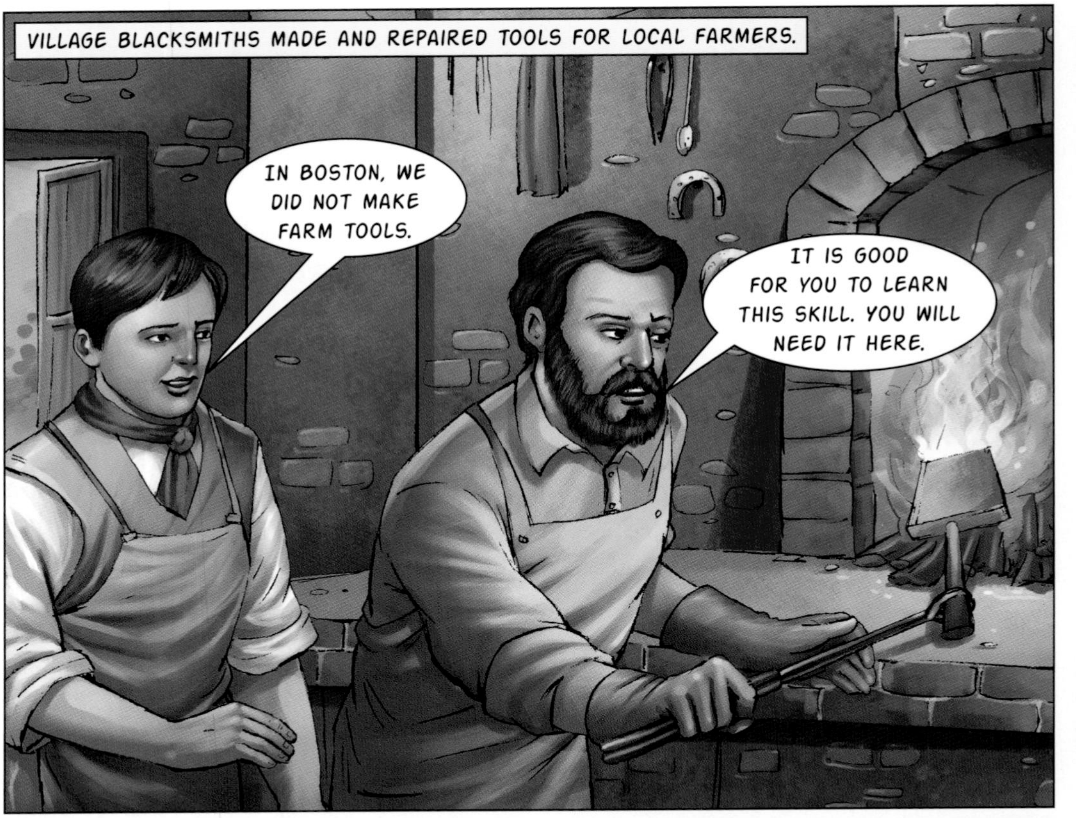
VILLAGE BLACKSMITHS MADE AND REPAIRED TOOLS FOR LOCAL FARMERS.
IN BOSTON, WE DID NOT MAKE FARM TOOLS.
IT IS GOOD FOR YOU TO LEARN THIS SKILL. YOU WILL NEED IT HERE.

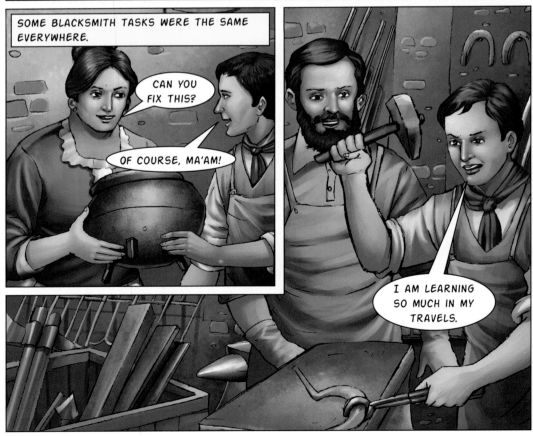

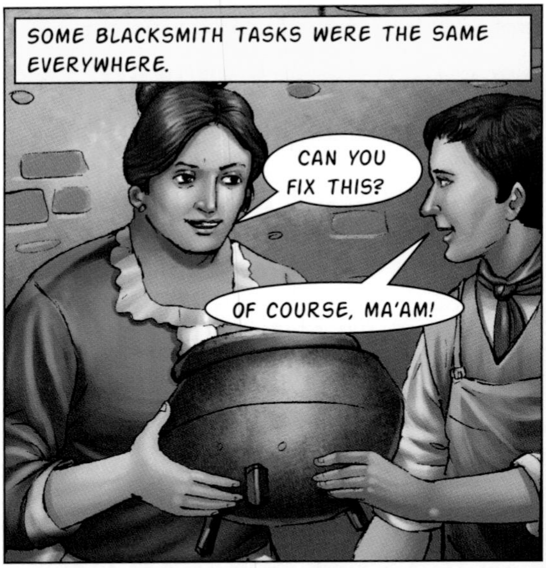
SOME BLACKSMITH TASKS WERE THE SAME EVERYWHERE.
CAN YOU FIX THIS?
OF COURSE, MA'AM!

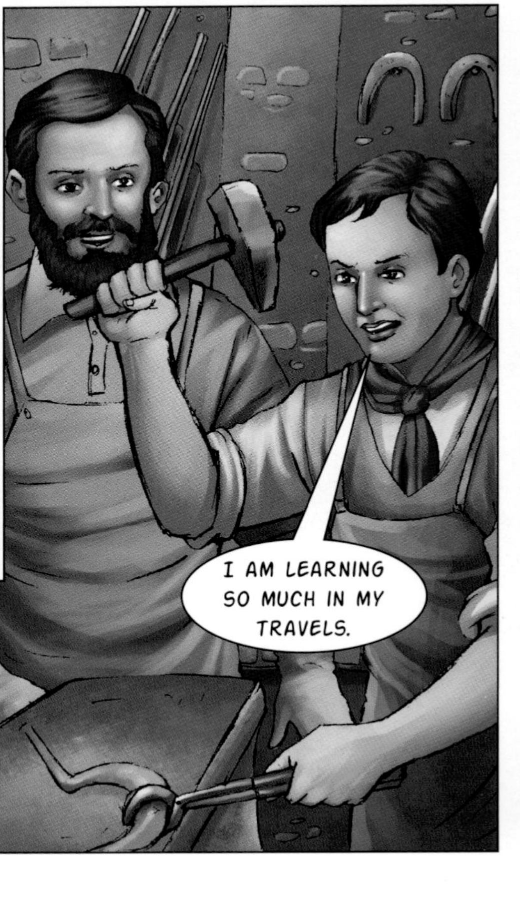
I AM LEARNING SO MUCH IN MY TRAVELS.

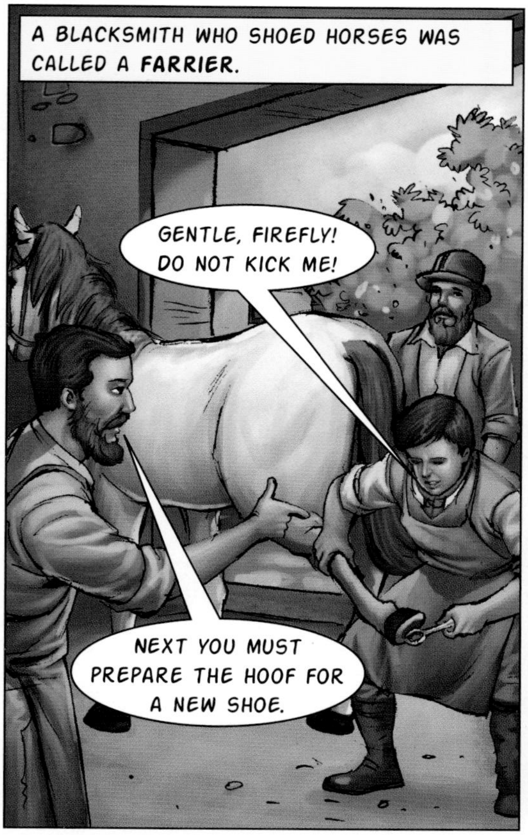
A BLACKSMITH WHO SHOED HORSES WAS CALLED A **FARRIER**.
GENTLE, FIREFLY! DO NOT KICK ME!
NEXT YOU MUST PREPARE THE HOOF FOR A NEW SHOE.

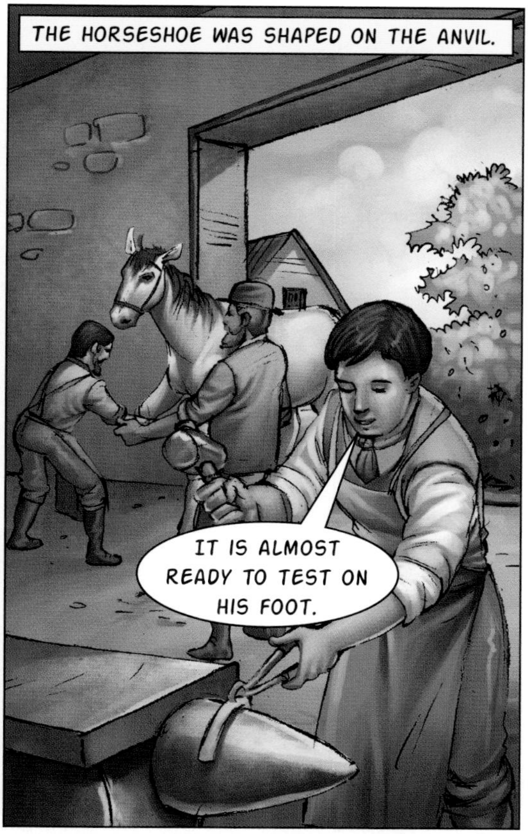
THE HORSESHOE WAS SHAPED ON THE ANVIL.
IT IS ALMOST READY TO TEST ON HIS FOOT.

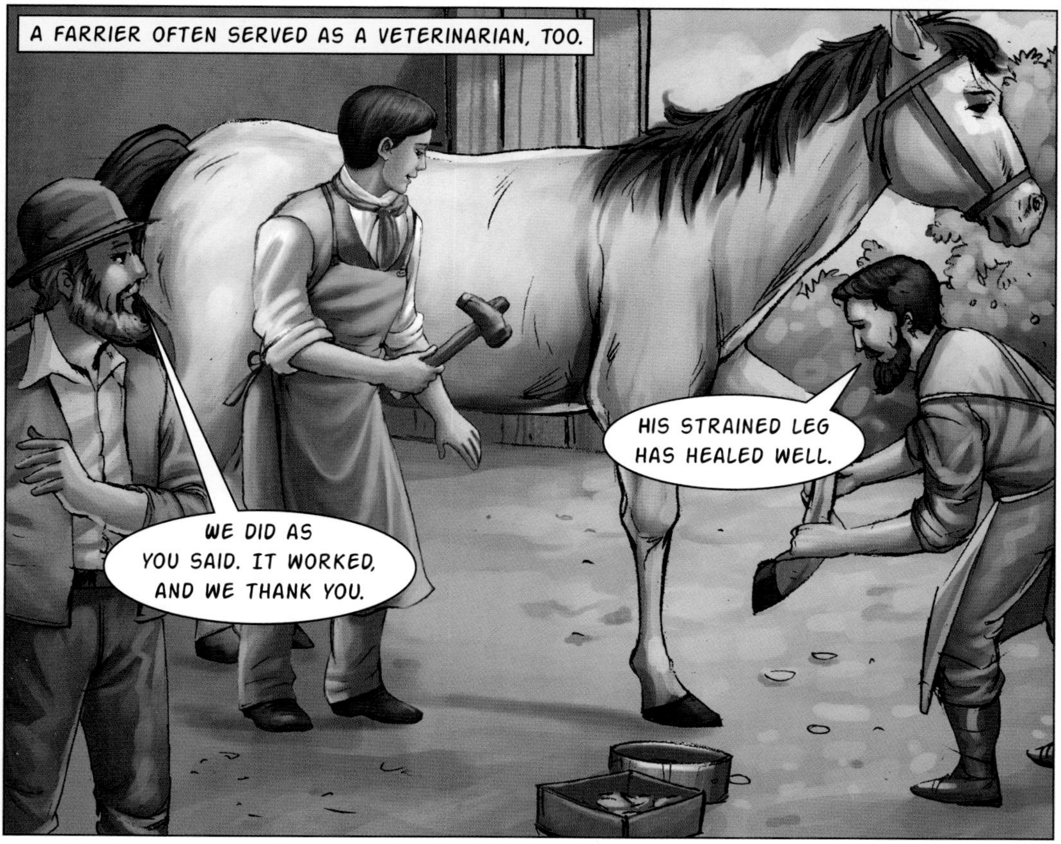
A FARRIER OFTEN SERVED AS A VETERINARIAN, TOO.
WE DID AS YOU SAID. IT WORKED, AND WE THANK YOU.
HIS STRAINED LEG HAS HEALED WELL.

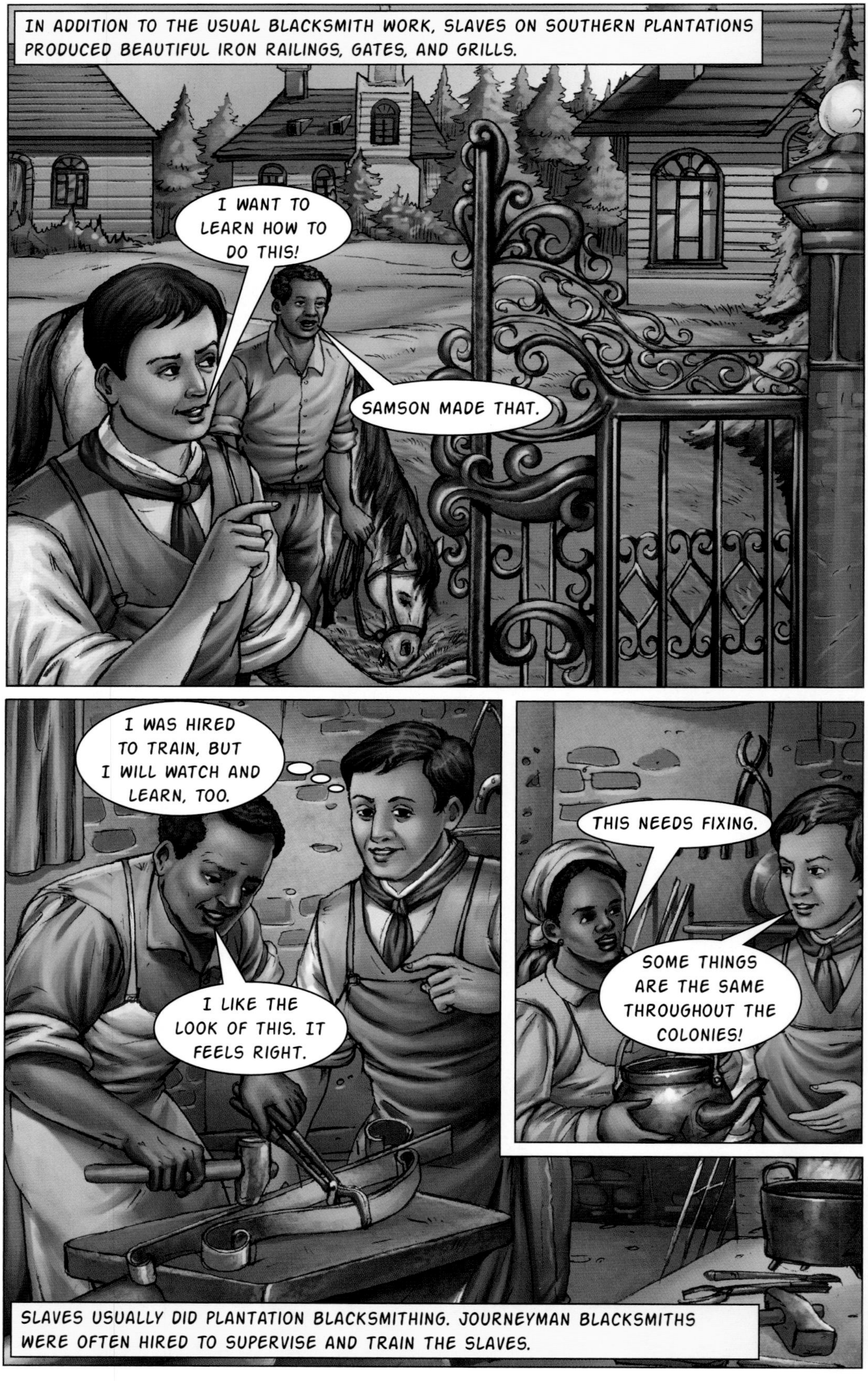
IN ADDITION TO THE USUAL BLACKSMITH WORK, SLAVES ON SOUTHERN PLANTATIONS PRODUCED BEAUTIFUL IRON RAILINGS, GATES, AND GRILLS.
I WANT TO LEARN HOW TO DO THIS!
SAMSON MADE THAT.
I WAS HIRED TO TRAIN, BUT I WILL WATCH AND LEARN, TOO.
I LIKE THE LOOK OF THIS. IT FEELS RIGHT.
THIS NEEDS FIXING.
SOME THINGS ARE THE SAME THROUGHOUT THE COLONIES!
SLAVES USUALLY DID PLANTATION BLACKSMITHING. JOURNEYMAN BLACKSMITHS WERE OFTEN HIRED TO SUPERVISE AND TRAIN THE SLAVES.

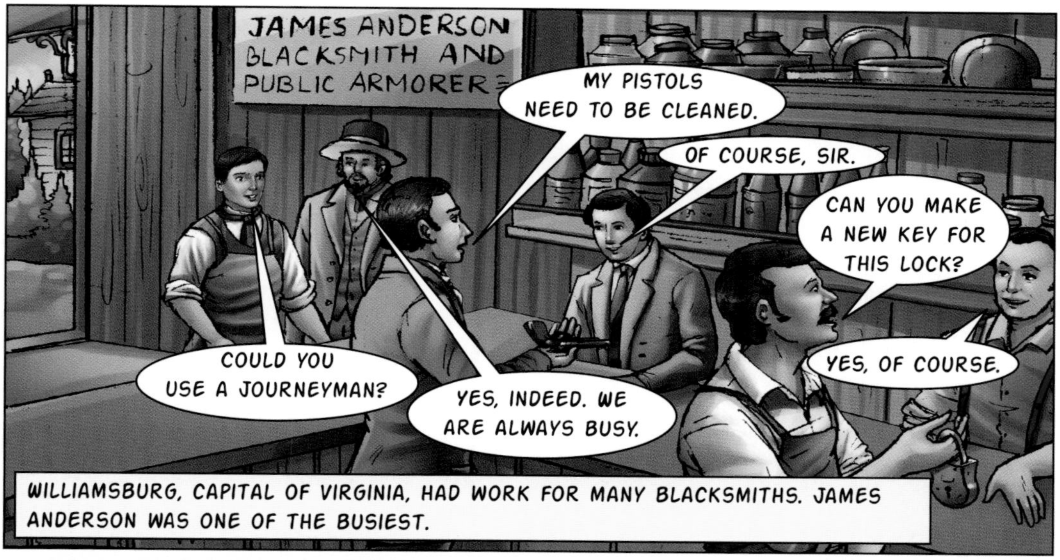
JAMES ANDERSON
BLACKSMITH AND
PUBLIC ARMORER
MY PISTOLS NEED TO BE CLEANED.
OF COURSE, SIR.
CAN YOU MAKE A NEW KEY FOR THIS LOCK?
YES, OF COURSE.
COULD YOU USE A JOURNEYMAN?
YES, INDEED. WE ARE ALWAYS BUSY.
WILLIAMSBURG, CAPITAL OF VIRGINIA, HAD WORK FOR MANY BLACKSMITHS. JAMES ANDERSON WAS ONE OF THE BUSIEST.

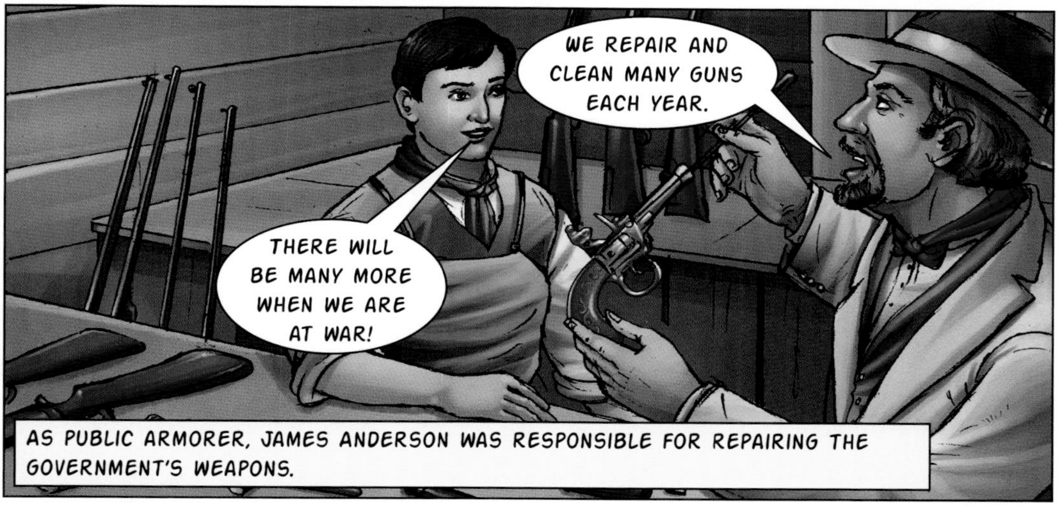
WE REPAIR AND CLEAN MANY GUNS EACH YEAR.
THERE WILL BE MANY MORE WHEN WE ARE AT WAR!
AS PUBLIC ARMORER, JAMES ANDERSON WAS RESPONSIBLE FOR REPAIRING THE GOVERNMENT'S WEAPONS.

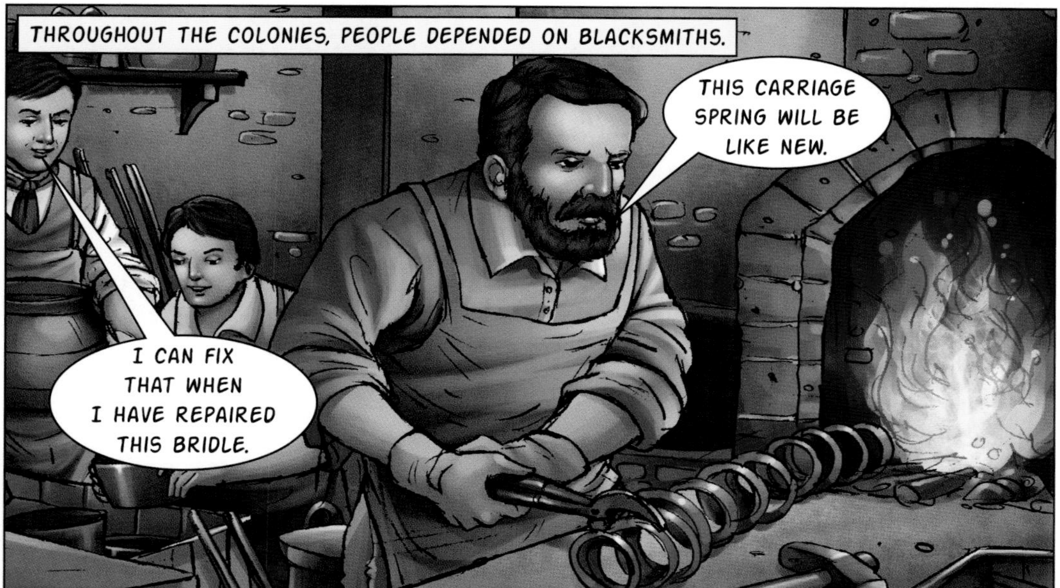
THROUGHOUT THE COLONIES, PEOPLE DEPENDED ON BLACKSMITHS.
THIS CARRIAGE SPRING WILL BE LIKE NEW.
I CAN FIX THAT WHEN I HAVE REPAIRED THIS BRIDLE.

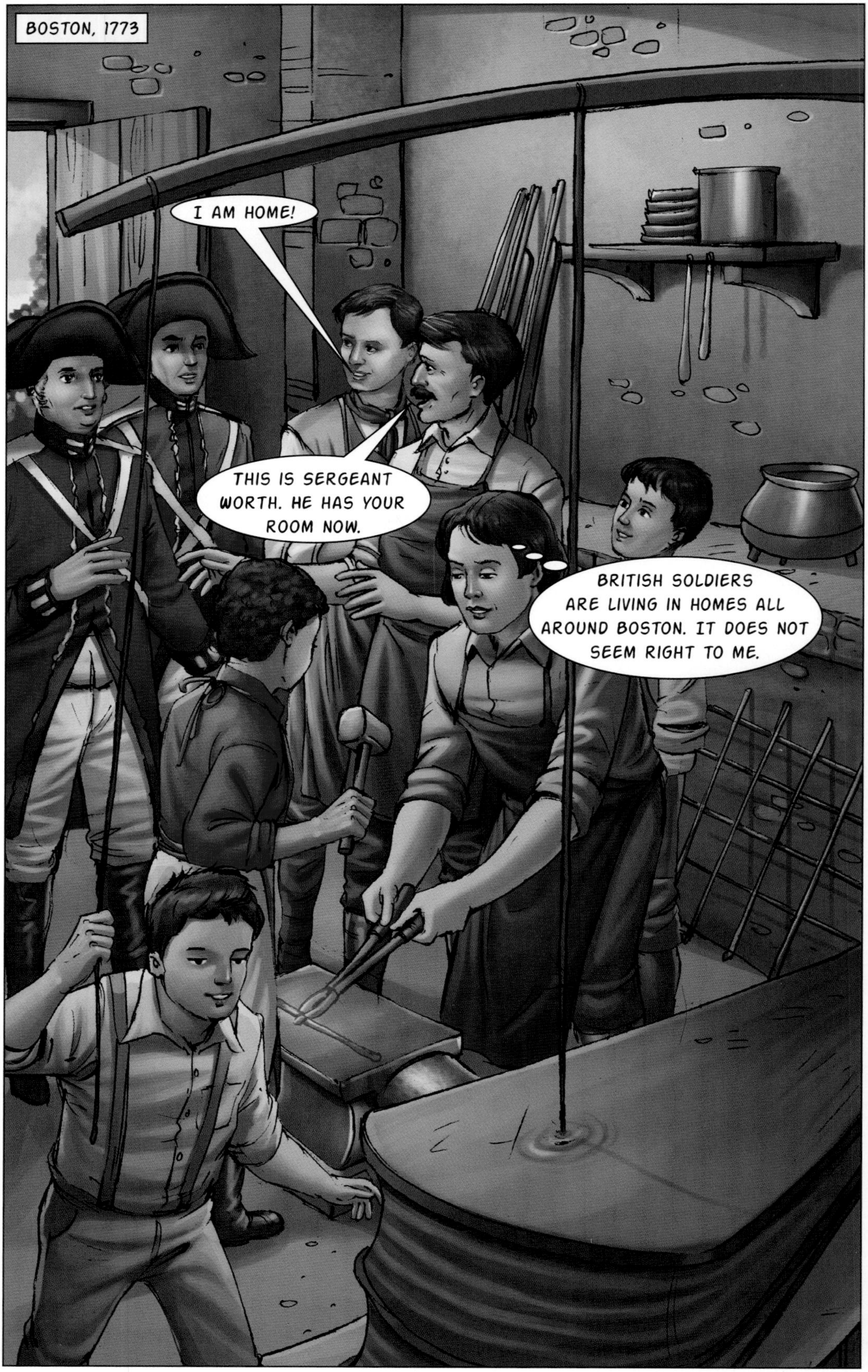
BOSTON, 1773
I AM HOME!
THIS IS SERGEANT WORTH. HE HAS YOUR ROOM NOW.
BRITISH SOLDIERS ARE LIVING IN HOMES ALL AROUND BOSTON. IT DOES NOT SEEM RIGHT TO ME.

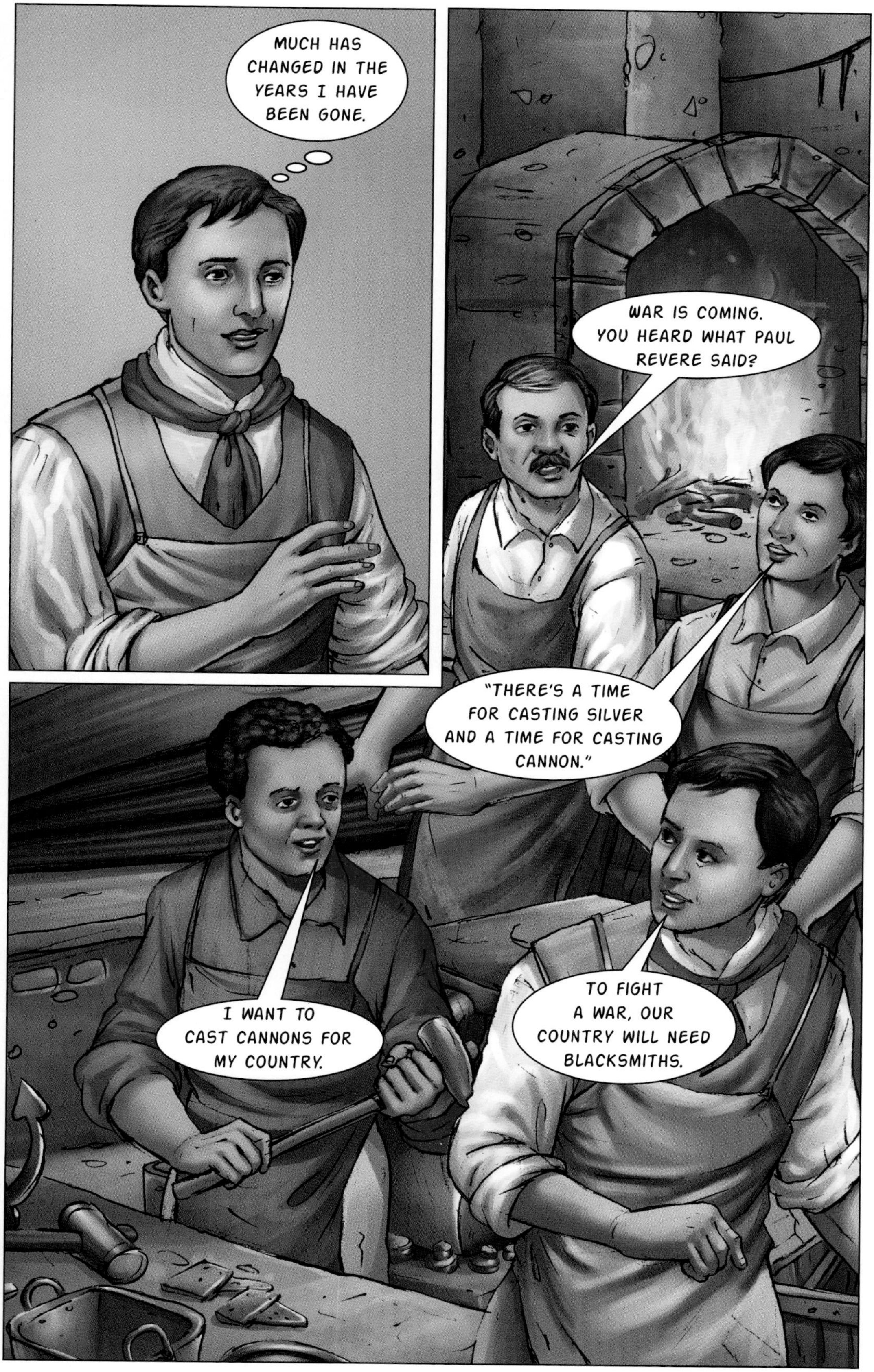
MUCH HAS CHANGED IN THE YEARS I HAVE BEEN GONE.
WAR IS COMING. YOU HEARD WHAT PAUL REVERE SAID?
"THERE'S A TIME FOR CASTING SILVER AND A TIME FOR CASTING CANNON."
I WANT TO CAST CANNONS FOR MY COUNTRY.
TO FIGHT A WAR, OUR COUNTRY WILL NEED BLACKSMITHS.

Famous Colonial Blacksmiths

Betsy Hager
(1750–1843)

Elizabeth "Betsy" Hager of Boston is best known for her work as a blacksmith during the American Revolution. She earned the nickname Betsy the Blacksmith by secretly restoring 60-year-old British muskets. Following the Battle of Concord, she repaired captured British cannons that were then used against the British. She also made bullets and other ammunition for use in the war.

Peter Townsend
(c. 1736–c. 1783)

New York blacksmith Peter Townsend is known for his role in producing a huge iron chain during the American Revolution. In February 1778, the Board of War asked Townsend to make a 500-yard- (457 m) long chain. It was to block the Hudson River at West Point, New York, and serve as a barrier to British vessels. Townsend hired 60 men, and the chain was finished in six weeks. Each link was 2 feet (1 m) long and weighed 114 pounds (52 kg). Installation of the 65-ton (59 t) Great Chain began on April 30, 1778, and it took 40 men four days to install it.

James Read
(? –1622)

James Read was among the first settlers to arrive in Jamestown, Virginia, in 1607. He was the town's only blacksmith and as such repaired and mended the early settlers' farm tools. Known for being rebellious and violent, he was sentenced to death for threatening the president of the colony. To save himself, he apologized and declared a conspiracy. His actions resulted in the execution of a town council member.

GLOSSARY

anvil (AN-vul) A large object on which metal is hammered into shapes.

apprentice (uh-PREN-tis) A person who learns a trade by working for someone who is already trained.

bellows (BEH-lohz) A bag with handles that lets out a flow of air when it is opened and closed.

blacksmiths (BLAK-smiths) People who make and fix iron objects.

bog iron (BOG EYE-urn) A deposit of impure limonite formed in marshy areas.

craftsmen (KRAFTS-men) Workmen who practice a certain trade.

farrier (FEHR-ee-er) A person who shoes horses.

forge (FORJ) A special kind of oven used by blacksmiths and other metalworkers to heat metal.

Iron Act (EYE-urn AKT) An act from 1750 permitting the colonies to supply only raw metals to England and prohibiting the manufacture of finished iron goods.

ironmongers (EYE-urn-mung-gurz) People who sell iron or metal tools.

journeyman (JER-nee-man) A worker who has learned a trade from one person but who works for another.

pig iron (PIG EYE-urn) Crude iron that comes out of the blast furnace and later is made into steel, wrought iron, or high-purity iron.

scrap iron (SKRAP EYE-urn) Rejected or discarded iron useful only as material for reprocessing.

smelting (SMEL-ting) Melting rock that contains metal in order to get the metal out.

vise (VYS) A device used to hold an item in place while it is being worked on. Vises are often attached to workbenches.

INDEX

WEBSITES

Due to the changing nature of Internet links, PowerKids Press has developed an online list of websites related to the subject of this book. This site is updated regularly. Please use this link to access the list:

www.powerkidslinks.com/jgca/smith/